THE BOOK OF COURAGE

MATTHEW KELLY

THE BOOK OF COURAGE

Beacon Publishing
P.O. Box 6366
Cincinnati, Ohio 45206
United States of America

Cover design: Wilker Design
Photography: Nathan Kelly

Library of Congress Cataloging-in Publication Data

Kelly, Matthew
The book of courage /
Matthew Kelly. - first edition
ISBN 1-929266-10-3 (cloth.)
1.Human Development. 2. Spirituality. 3. Recovery.
4. Kelly, Matthew.
I Title.

03 04 05 06 07 · 10 9 8 7 6 5 4 3 2 1

Over the past three years I have lost three people very
dear to me to cancer. This mysterious disease is
becoming more and more common.
We don't know what causes it,
we don't how to cure it,
but we all know people who are suffering from it.

I would like to dedicate this book
to my father — Bernard Kelly
to my friends — Jim Willig and Karen Berry,
and
to the millions of people around the world
who suffer torturous pain
and anguish everyday
at the hands of the tyrant
we call Cancer.

— MATTHEW KELLY —

EVERYTHING IN LIFE REQUIRES COURAGE. Whether it is playing football, or coaching football; crossing the room to ask a woman out on a date, or rekindling a love that has grown cold; whether it's your first day at college, or your first day back at college after twenty years; starting a new business, battling a potentially fatal disease, getting married, struggling to overcome an addiction, or coming humbly before your God in prayer: life takes courage.

Courage is essential to the human experience. Courage animates us, brings us to life, and makes everything else possible. And yet, courage is the rarest quality in the human person.

The most dominant emotion today in our modern society is fear. We are afraid. Afraid of losing the things we have worked hard to buy, afraid of rejection and failure, afraid of certain parts of town, afraid of certain types of people, afraid of criticism, afraid of suffering and heartache, afraid of change, afraid to tell people how we really feel... We are afraid of so many things. We are even afraid to be ourselves. Some of these fears we are consciously aware of, while others exist sub-consciously. But these fears can play a very large role in directing the actions and activities of our lives. Fear has a tendency to imprison us. Fear stops more people from doing something with their lives than lack of ability, contacts, resources, or any other single variable. Fear paralyses the human spirit.

Courage is not the absence of fear, but the acquired ability to move beyond fear. Each day we must pass through the jungles of doubt and cross the valley of fear. For it is only then that we can live in the high-places — on the peaks of courage.

Take a moment to wander through the pages of history — your family's history, your nation's history, human history — and extract from those pages the men and women whom you most admire. What would they be without courage? Nothing worthwhile in history is achieved without courage. Courage is the father of every great moment and movement in history.

I have felt the chilling winds of fear and self-doubt rush against my skin. I have discovered that courage is learning to recognize and master that single moment. That moment is a prelude. A prelude to courage, or a prelude to fear. So much can be accomplished in one moment of courage. And so much can be lost to one moment of fear.

No one is born with courage. It is an acquired virtue. You learn to ride a bicycle by riding a bicycle. You learn to dance by dancing. You learn to play football by playing football. Courage is acquired by practicing courage. And like most qualities of character, when practiced our courage becomes stronger and more readily accessible with each passing day.

HOW I WISH I COULD SIT DOWN WITH MICHELANGELO, Abraham Lincoln, Shakespeare, Joan of Arc, Michael Jordan, Mother Teresa, Ghandi, John Paul II, Martin Luther King, Albert Einstein, Socrates, and wasting no time, ask them to share with me the passions and principles of their extraordinary lives. If I could sit down and talk to these people and you could sit nearby and eavesdrop on our conversations — the contents of this book is what you would hear.

I was seventeen years old when my love for quotes was ignited. I remember the day as if it were yesterday. My high school friend, Luke Herro, gave me a large photo of Albert Einstein with the quote, "Imagination is more important than knowledge" inscribed underneath the picture. I read that quote, and re-read that quote, over and over, and over again. I questioned whether it was true, I reflected on what it meant to my life, and I wondered what it meant to Einstein.

Since that day more than ten years ago, I have collected the quotes that make up this book. They are excerpts from the writings of men and women who have lived in various places at various times. They are words that have challenged and inspired me to embark on the adventure of life more courageously. It is my hope that they will serve you in the same way.

The words that fill the pages of this book represent thousands of years of wisdom, but just like the words that fill other books, they are just words until we decide to allow them to transform our lives. I encourage you to ponder each of these quotes over and over in relation to the various aspects of your life. Slowly. Thoughtfully. If you don't understand a quote, pass on to the next. If you disagree with one, pass on to the next. Allow the waters of time to pass under the bridge of your life, and perhaps when you return to those quotes, you will have a new perspective.

HAVE YOU EVER BEEN AWOKEN IN THE MORNING by the alarm clock in the middle of a wonderful dream? What happens? You try to go back to sleep. Maybe you can and maybe you can't get back to sleep, but what doesn't happen? The dream doesn't return. Life is that dream.

If you knew one year from today you were going to die, what would you do with the next year of your life? Do those things. Go home tonight and make a list. Then set about making those things happen. Revisit that list every-day, check on your progress, and renew your resolution. Use the words in this book each day to inspire you to make them happen. Life is short and you are dead an awful long time. Live life passionately. Laugh often, love always, cultivate soul, don't be afraid to dream the big dreams, and embrace your God.

Our world is changing so quickly. It can be a little frightening at times. It is easy to become so busy worrying about the future that we forget to live our dreams. There is something wonderful about a dream. It is not the achievement of the dream that matters most, but rather the pursuit of those dreams that are born from deep within us. The pursuit of the dream is life. Pursuing dreams does something mysterious to us. It fills us with hope, passion, and enthusiasm, and expands our capacities as a human person in every way.

So what are we waiting for? We only get one shot at life. Isn't it time for a little soul-searching? Visit a quiet church in the middle of the day. Take a walk in the park. Turn off the television and talk to your children. Open the paper and look for the job you've always wanted. Keep a promise. Tell your mom you love her. Restore an old Ford. Make friends with your neighbors. Say yes instead of maybe. Watch a sunset. Write your spouse a love letter. Fly a kite. Say "sorry". Ask that girl out on a date. Try a food you've never tasted before. Make peace with God.

Don't waste your life, because life is there — all you have to do is reach out and embrace it. Anything is possible. Whatever your dream is, make it happen. Have courage. Start today. You will be amazed what life will give you in return for a little bit of courage.

Be certain of one thing, the measure of your life will be the measure of your courage.

He who loses wealth
loses much;
he who loses a friend
loses more;
but he who loses courage
loses all.

— Cervantes —

Our deepest fear is not that we are inadequate.
Our deepest fear is that we are powerful beyond
measure. It is our light, not our darkness, that
most frightens us. We ask ourselves, who am I to
be brilliant, gorgeous, talented and fabulous?
Actually, who are you not to be? You are a child
of God. Your playing small doesn't serve the
world. There is nothing enlightened about
shrinking so that other people won't feel insecure
around you. We are born to make manifest the
glory of God that is within us. It is not just in some
of us, it is in everyone. And as we let our own
light shine, we unconsciously give other people
permission to do the same. As we are liberated
from our own fear, our presence automatically
liberates others.

— Nelson Mandela —

"Come to the edge," he said.
They said, "We are afraid."
"Come to the edge," he said again.
They came.
He pushed them... and they flew.

— Guillaume Apollinaire —

Whatever you do, you need courage.
Whatever course you decide upon, there is
always someone to tell you that you are
wrong. There are always difficulties arising
that tempt you to believe your critics are
right. To map a course of action and follow
it to an end requires some of the same
courage that a soldier needs. Peace has its
victories, but it takes brave men and
women to win them.

— Ralph Waldo Emerson —

A great deal of talent is lost to the world for want of a little courage. Every day sends to their graves obscure men whose timidity prevented them from making a first effort.

— Sydney Smith —

You gain strength, courage, and
confidence by every experience
in which you really stop to look fear
in the face. You are able to say to
yourself, "I lived through this horror.
I can take the next thing that
comes along..." We must do the
things we think we cannot.

— Eleanor Roosevelt —

The greater danger for most of us is not
that our aim is too high and we miss it,
but that it is too low and we reach it.

— Michelangelo —

I know this now. Every man gives his life for what he believes. Every woman gives her life for what she believes. Sometimes people believe in little or nothing, and yet they give their lives to that little or nothing.
One life is all we have and we live it as we believe in living it and then it's gone. But to surrender what you are and to live without belief is more terrible than dying — even more terrible than dying young.

— Joan of Arc —

Be bold and courageous.
When you look back on your life,
you'll regret the things you didn't do
more than the ones you did.

— H. Jackson Brown Jr. —

The most secret, sacred wish that lies deep down at the bottom of your heart, the wonderful thing that you hardly dare to look at, or think about — the thing that you would rather die than have anyone else know of, because it seems so far beyond anything that you are, or have at the present time, that you fear that you would be cruelly ridiculed if the mere thought of it were known — that is just the very thing that God is wishing you to do or to be for him. And the birth of that marvelous wish in your soul — the dawning of that secret dream — was the Voice of God himself telling you to arise and come up higher because he had need of you.

— Emmet Fox —

If one advances confidently in the
endeavors to live the life which he has
imagined, he will meet with a success
unexpected in common hours.

— Henry David Thoreau —

The more faithfully you listen to
the voice within you,
the better you will hear what
is sounding outside of you.

— Dag Hammarskjold —

First do what is necessary,
then do what is possible,
and before long
you will find yourself
doing the impossible.

— Francis of Assisi —

The shortest and surest way to live with
honor in the world is to be in reality what we
would appear to be; all human virtues
increase and strengthen themselves by the
practice and experience of them.

— Socrates —

COURAGE… It's just another word for inner strength, presence of mind against odds, determination to hang in there, to venture, persevere, and withstand hardship. It's got keeping power… It's what makes the amputee reject pity and continue to take life by the throat. It's what forces every married couple having trouble never to say, "Let's terminate." It's what encourages the divorcee to face tomorrow. It's what upholds the young mother with kids in spite of a personal energy crisis… Every day, in some way, your courage will be tested. Your test may be as simple as saying, "No," as uneventful as facing a pile of dirty laundry, or as unknown and unheralded as an inner struggle between right and wrong. God's medal-of-honor winners are made in secret because most of their courageous acts occur deep down inside.

— Charles R. Swindoll —

Have courage for the great sorrows of life
and patience for the small ones;
and when you have laboriously accomplished
your daily task, go to sleep in peace.
God is awake.

— Victor Hugo —

The older I get, the more wisdom I find in the
ancient rule of taking first things first — a
process which often reduces the most
complex human problems
to manageable proportions.

— Dwight D. Eisenhower —

Courage is being scared
to death — and saddling
up anyway.

— John Wayne —

Be patient toward all that is unresolved in your
heart. And try to love the questions themselves.
Do not seek the answers that cannot be given
you because you would not be able to live them.
And the point is to live everything. Live the
questions now. Perhaps you will then
gradually, without noticing it, live along
some distant day into the answer.

— Rainer Maria Rilke —

One can choose to go back toward
safety or forward toward growth.
Growth must be chosen again
and again; fear must be
overcome again and again.

— Abraham Maslow —

There is a time for departure
even when there is no
certain place to go.

— Tennessee Williams —

We must never forget that today's
legendary achievements — awesome as
they may seem — were yesterday's risky
adventures. Courage is not the capacity never
to be afraid; as Karl Barth reminds us,
"Courage is fear that has said its prayers."

— John R. Claypool —

We are not human beings
having a spiritual experience.
We are spiritual beings
having a human experience.

— Pierre Teilhard De Chardin —

I believe that nothing that happens to me is meaningless, and that it is good for us all that it should be so, even if it runs counter to our own wishes. As I see it, I'm here for some purpose, and I only hope I may fulfill it. In the light of the great purpose all our privations and disappointments are trivial.

— Dietrich Bonhoeffer —

Life is meant to be lived from a Center, a divine Center...
There is a divine Abyss within us all, a holy Infinite
Center, a Heart, a Life who speaks in us and through us to
the world. We have all heard this holy Whisper at times.
At times we have followed the Whisper, an amazing
equilibrium of life, amazing effectiveness of living set in.
But too many of us have heeded the Voice only at
times... We have not counted this Holy Thing within us
to be the most precious thing in the world.

— Thomas R. Kelly —

Learn to say no.
It will be of more use to you
than to be able to read Latin.

— Charles Haddon Spurgeon —

People can succeed at almost
anything for which they
have unlimited enthusiasm.

— Charles Schwab —

To be glad of life because it gives you a chance to love and work and to play and to look up at the stars — to be satisfied with your possessions but not contented with yourself until you have made the best of them — to despise nothing in the world except falsehood and meanness, and to fear nothing except cowardice — to be governed by your admirations rather than by your disgusts; to covet nothing that is your neighbor's except his kindness of heart and gentleness of manners — to think seldom of your enemies, often of your friends, and everyday of Christ; and to spend as much time as you can, with body and with spirit, in God's out-of-doors — these are little guide-posts on the foot-path to peace.

— Henry Van Dyke —

It's when we're given a choice
that we sit with God and
design ourselves.

— Dorothy Gilman —

The great French Marshall Lyautey
once asked his gardener to plant a tree.
The gardener objected that the tree
was slow growing and would not reach
maturity for 100 years. The Marshall replied,
"In that case, there is no time to lose;
plant it this afternoon."

— John F. Kennedy —

Often the difference between a successful man
and a failure is not one's better abilities or ideas,
but the courage that one has to bet on his ideas,
to take a calculated risk — and to act.

— Maxwell Maltz —

Life is either a daring adventure or nothing.
Security does not exist in nature, nor do the
children of men as a whole experience it.
Avoiding danger is no safer in the
long run than exposure.

— Helen Keller —

Whatever you can do,
or dream you can,
begin it.
Boldness has genius,
power, and magic in it.
Begin it now.

— Goethe —

Place your talents and enthusiasm
at the service of life.

— Pope John Paul II —

Our doubts are traitors,
and make us lose the good
we oft might win
by fearing to attempt.

— William Shakespeare —

A journey of a thousand miles
begins with a single step.

— Lao Tzu —

Life's greatest happiness
is to be convinced that we are loved.

— Victor Hugo —

Men acquire a particular quality by
constantly acting in a particular way.

— Aristotle —

A leader is useless when he acts against
the prompting of his own conscience,
surrounded as he must be by people holding
all kinds of views.
He will drift like an anchorless ship if he has not
the inner voice to hold him firm and guide him.

— Ghandi —

Everything is possible
for the one who believes.

— Jesus of Nazareth —

Some people are going to like me
and some people aren't, so I might as
well be me.
Then, at least, I will know that the
people who like me, like me.

— Hugh Prather —

Some men see things as they are
and say, "why?"
I dream things that never were
and say, "Why not?"

— Robert F. Kennedy —

We may affirm absolutely that nothing
great in the world has been
accomplished without passion.

— Hegel —

The number of needless tasks
that are performed daily
by thousands of people
is amazing.

— Henry Ford —

The dictionary is the only place that success
comes before work. Hard work is the price
we must pay for success. I think you can
accomplish almost anything if you're
willing to pay the price.

— Vince Lombardi —

If a man does not keep pace with his companions,
perhaps it is because he hears a different
drummer. Let him step to the music which he
hears, however measured and far away.

— Henry David Thoreau —

Courage and perseverance have a magical
tailsman, before which difficulties
disappear and obstacles vanish into air.

— John Quincy Adams —

I've missed more than 9,000 shots in my career, I've lost more than 300 games, and 26 times I've been trusted to take the game winning shot and missed. Throughout my life and career I've failed, and failed, and failed again. And, that's why I succeed.

— Michael Jordan —

Quiet minds
cannot be perplexed or frightened,
but go on in fortune or misfortune
at their own private pace,
like a clock during a thunder storm.

— Robert Louis Stevenson —

I have watched men climb up to success, hundreds of them, and of all the elements that are important for success, the most important is faith. No great thing comes to any man unless he has courage.

— James Cardinal Gibbons —

I find the great thing in this world is not
so much where we stand as in what
direction we are moving.

— Oliver Wendell Holmes —

They can because they think they can.

— Virgil —

The strong, calm man is always loved and revered.
He is like a shade-giving tree in a thirsty land, or a
sheltering rock in a storm. Who does not love a tranquil
heart, a sweet-tempered, balanced life? It does not matter
if it rains or shines, or what changes come to
those possessing these blessings, for they are
always sweet, serene, and calm. That exquisite poise of
character which we call serenity is the last lesson of
culture; it is the flowering of life, the fruitage of the soul. It
is precious as wisdom, more to be desired than
gold - yea, than even fine gold. How insignificant mere
money-seeking looks in comparison with a serene life - a
life that dwells in the ocean of Truth, beneath the waves,
beyond the reach of tempests, in the Eternal Calm!

— James Allen —

The privilege of a lifetime is being
who you are.

— Joseph Campbell —

The key is to keep company only with
people who uplift you, whose presence
calls forth your best.

— Epictetus —

Courage is the most important of all virtues,
because without courage, you cannot
practice any of the other virtues consistently.

— Maya Angelou —

A ship in port is safe, but that is not
what ships are built for.

— Benazir Bhutto —

I have learned over the years that when one's mind is made up, this diminishes fear; knowing what must be done goes away with fear.

— Rosa Parks —

The more one does and sees and feels, the more one is able to do, and the more genuine may be one's appreciation of fundamental things like home, and love, and understanding companionship.

— Amelia Earhart —

I long to accomplish a great and noble task, but it is my chief duty to accomplish humble tasks as though they were great and noble. The world is moved along, not only by the mighty shoves of its heroes, but also by the aggregate of the tiny pushes of each honest worker.

— Helen Keller —

He who every morning plans the transactions of the day and follows out that plan carries a thread that will guide him through the labyrinth of the most busy life. The orderly arrangement of his time is like a ray of light which darts itself through all his occupations. But where no plan is laid, where the disposal of time is surrendered merely to the chance of incidents, chaos will soon reign.

— Victor Hugo —

All men should strive to learn before
they die what they are running from,
and to, and why.

— James Thurber —

I think that, regardless of our culture, age, or even personal handicaps, we can still strive for something exceptional. Why not expand our sights instead of restricting our lives and accepting the lowest common denominator of a dormant existence? Faith… will permit us to take a chance on a new path, perhaps different from the one we now follow. It may be surprising where it leads.

— Jimmy Carter —

I don't know the key to success,
but the key to failure is trying
to please everybody.

— Bill Cosby —

We who lived in concentration camps can remember the men who walked through the huts comforting others, giving away their last piece of bread. They may have been few in number, but they offer sufficient proof that everything can be taken from a man but one thing: the last of the human freedoms — to choose one's attitude in any given set of circumstances — to choose one's own way.

— Victor Frankl —

In the depth of winter I finally learned
that within me there lay and
invincible summer.

— Albert Camus —

All our dreams can come true — if we
have the courage to pursue them.

— Walt Disney —

There is a pervasive form of contemporary violence to which the idealist fighting for peace by nonviolent methods most easily succumbs: activism and overwork. The rush and pressure of modern life are a form, perhaps the most common form, of its innate violence. To allow oneself to be carried away by a multitude of conflicting concerns, to surrender to too many projects, to want to help everyone in everything is to succumb to violence. The frenzy of the activist neutralizes one's work for peace. It destroys the fruitfulness of one's work, because it kills the root of inner wisdom which makes work fruitful.

— Thomas Merton —

We must be willing to get rid of the life
we've planned, so as to have the life
that is waiting for us.

— Joseph Campbell —

You don't get to choose how you're going to die. Or when. You can only decide how you're going to live. Now.

— Joan Baez —

Procrastination is the fear of success. People procrastinate because they are afraid of the success that they know will result if they move ahead now. Because success is heavy, carries a responsibility with it, and requires an individual to continue to set an example, it is much easier to procrastinate and live on the "Someday I'll" philosophy.

Winners don't live their lives in the future, safely out of sight. They set goals in the specific, foreseeable future, which gives their everyday activities richness and purpose.

— Denis Waitley —

I never take counsel of my fears.

— General George Patton —

It's surprising how many people go through life
without ever recognizing that their feelings
toward other people are largely determined by
their feelings toward themselves, and if you're not
comfortablc with yourself, you can't be
comfortable with others.

— Sydney J. Harris —

People who are unable to motivate themselves
must be content with mediocrity, no matter
how impressive their other talents.

— Andrew Carnegie —

The most rewarding things you do in life
are often the ones that look like
they can't be done.

— Arnold Palmer —

Men stumble over the truth from time to time, but most pick themselves up and hurry off as if nothing happened.

— Winston Churchill —

Nobody grows old by merely living a number of years. People grow old only by deserting their ideals. Years wrinkle the face, but to give up enthusiasm wrinkles the soul. Worry, doubt, self-interest, fear, despair — these are the long, long years that bow the head and turn the growing spirit back to dust.

— Watterson Lowe —

Ordinary people merely think how they shall spend their time; a man of talent tries to use it.

— Arthur Schopenhauer —

We shall steer safely through every storm, so
long as our heart is right, our intention fervent,
our courage steadfast, and our trust fixed on
God. If at times we are somewhat stunned
by the tempest, never fear. Let us take breath,
and go on afresh.

— Francis de Sales —

A man would do nothing if he waited until
he could do it so well that no one would
find fault with what he has done.

— John Henry Newman —

The true worth of a man is to be measured
by the things he pursues.

— Marcus Aurelius —

Don't be afraid to take a big step if one is
indicated. You can't cross a chasm in
two small jumps.

— David Lloyd George —

The ancestor of every action
is thought.

— Ralph Waldo Emerson —

Do what you can,
with what you have,
where you are.

— Theodore Roosevelt —

They always say that time changes things,
but actually you have to change
them yourself.

— Andy Warhol —

Remember you have only one soul; that you have only one death to die; that you have only one life, which is short and has to be lived by you alone; and there is only one glory, which is eternal. If you do this, there will be a great many things about which you care nothing.

— Teresa of Avila —

Life shrinks or expands in proportion
to one's courage.

— Anais Nin —

Man cannot discover new oceans until he has the courage to lose sight of the shore.

— Anon —

Everyone has talent. What is rare is the courage to follow that talent to the dark place where it leads.

— Erica Jong —

Courage is resistance to fear,
mastery of fear, not absence of fear.

— Mark Twain —

.

Courage is fear holding on
one minute longer.

— General George Patton —

Neither a borrower, nor a lender be:
For loan oft loses both itself and friend,
And borrowing dulls the edge of husbandry.
This above all; to thine own self be true,
And it must follow, as the night follows the day,
Thou canst not then be false to any man.

— William Shakespeare —

Imagination is more important
than knowledge.

— Albert Einstein —

As long as you keep a person down,
some part of you has to be down there to
hold him down, so it means you cannot
soar as you otherwise might.

— Marian Anderson —

When we listen with the intent to understand others, rather than with the intent to reply, we begin true communication and relationship building. Opportunities to then speak openly and to be understood come much more naturally and easily. Seeking to understand takes consideration; seeking to be understood takes courage. Effectiveness lies in balancing the two.

— Stephen R. Covey —

I have found that among its other benefits, giving liberates
the soul of the giver... When we cast our bread upon the
waters, we can presume that someone downstream whose
face we will never know will benefit from our action, as we
who are downstream from another will profit from that
grantor's gift. Our bounty, once decided upon, should be
without concern, overflowing one minute and forgotten the
next... When we give cheerfully and accept gratefully,
everyone is blessed.

— Maya Angelou —

A keen sense of humor helps us to overlook the unbecoming, understand the unconventional, tolerate the unpleasant, overcome the unexpected, and outlast the unbearable.

— Billy Graham —

The secret of success is to make your
vocation your vacation.

— Mark Twain —

When we think about the people who have given us hope
and have increased the strength of our soul, we might
discover that they were not advice givers, warners, or
moralists, but the few who were able to articulate in words
and actions the human condition in which we participate...
Not because of any solution they offered but because of the
courage to enter so deeply into human suffering and speak
from there. Neither Kirkegaard nor Satre nor Camus nor
Hammarskjold nor Solzhenitsyn has offered solutions, but
many who read their words find new strength to pursue
their own personal search. Those who do not run away
from our pains but touch them with compassion bring
healing and new strength... In our solution-oriented world it
is more important than ever to realize that wanting to
alleviate pain without sharing it is like wanting to save a
child from a burning house without the risk of being hurt.

— Henri Nouwen —

He who is not courageous enough to take risks will accomplish nothing in life.

— Muhammad Ali —

God does not die on the day when we cease to
believe in a personal deity, but we die on the day
when our lives cease to be illumined by the steady
radiance, renewed daily of a wonder, the source
of which is beyond all reason.

— Dag Hammarskjold —

My obligation is to do the right thing.
The rest is in God's hands.

— Martin Luther King —

I read and walked for miles at night
along the beach, writing bad blank verse
and searching endlessly
for someone wonderful who
would step out of the darkness
and change my life.
It never crossed my mind that that person
could be me.

— Anna Quindlen —

Why is it so hard for so many to realize
that winners are usually the ones
who work harder, work longer and, as a result,
perform better?

— John Wooden —

Man cannot do right in one department of life
whilst he is occupied in doing wrong in another
department. Life is one indivisible whole.

— Ghandi —

I said to the almond tree, "Sister, speak to me of God," and the almond tree blossomed.

— Greco —

It is not the critic that counts; nor the man who points out how the strong man stumbled or where the doer of deeds could have done them better. The credit belongs to the man who is actually in the arena; whose face is marred by dust and sweat and blood; who strives valiantly; who errs, and comes short again and again, because there is no effort without error and shortcomings, who does actually try to do the deed; who knows the great enthusiasm, the great devotion, and spends himself in a worthy cause; who, at worst, if he fails, at least fails while daring greatly. Far better it is to dare mighty things, to win glorious triumphs even though checkered by failure, than to rank among those timid souls who neither enjoy nor suffer much, because they live in the gray twilight that knows neither victory nor defeat.

— Theodore Roosevelt —

The chemist who can extract from his heart's elements compassion, respect, longing, patience, regret, surprise, and forgiveness and compound them into one can create that atom which is called love.

— Kahlil Gibran —

It's a funny thing about life; if you refuse to accept anything but the best, you very often get it.

— W. Somerset Maugham —

There is only one success — to be able to spend your life in your own way.

— Christopher Morley —

Every now and then go away, have a little relaxation, for when you come back to your work your judgement will be surer; since to remain constantly at work will cause you to lose power of judgement …

Go some distance away because the work appears smaller and more of it can be taken in at a glance, and a lack of harmony or proportion is more readily seen.

— Leonardo da Vinci —

I went to the woods because I wanted to live
deliberately… I wanted to live deep and suck
out all of the marrow of life! To put to rout all
that was not life. And not, when I came to
die, discover that I had not lived…

— Henry David Thoreau —

I hear and I forget.
I see and I remember.
I do and I understand.

— Chinese Proverb —

True silence is the rest of the mind; it is to the spirit what sleep is to the body, nourishment and refreshment.

— William Penn —

What lies behind us and what lies before us
are small matters compared to what lies
within us.

— Ralph Waldo Emerson —

Genius is eternal patience.

— Michelangelo —

It is better to light one small candle
than to curse the darkness.

— Confucius —

In the long run, men hit only what they aim at. Therefore… they had better aim at something high.

— Henry David Thoreau —

Courage is a special kind of knowledge:
the knowledge of how to fear what ought
to be feared and how not to fear what
ought not to be feared.

— David Ben-Gurion —

The soul is healed by
being with children.

— Fyodor Dostoyevski —

People are always blaming circumstances for
what they are. I don't believe in circumstances.
The people who get on in this world are the
people who get up and look for the
circumstances they want, and, if they
can't find them, make them.

— George Bernard Shaw —

During the past thirty years, people from all civilized
countries of the earth have consulted me. I have treated
many hundreds of patients. Among all my patients in the
second half of life — that is to say, over thirty-five — there
has not been one whose problem in the last resort was not
that of finding a religious outlook on life. It is safe to say that
every one of them fell ill because he had lost that which the
living religions of every age have given to their followers,
and none of them has been really healed who did not
regain his religious outlook.

— Carl Jung —

Do not let your life
be like a shooting star which lights up the sky
for only a brief moment.
Let your life be like the sun that always burns brightly
in the heavens
bringing light and warmth to all those on Earth.
Let your light shine!

— Matthew Kelly —

To seek God, one need not go on a pilgrimage
or light lamps fed with ghee and burn incense
before the image of the deity or anoint it or
paint it with vermilion. For He resides in our
hearts. If we could humbly obliterate in us
the consciousness of our physical body,
we would see Him face to face.

— Ghandi —

Men make history, and not the other way
around. In periods where there is no
leadership, society stands still. Progress
occurs when courageous, skillful leaders
seize the opportunity to change things
for the better.

— Harry S. Truman —

The unexamined life is not worth living.

— Socrates —

We are what we repeatedly do.
Excellence, then, is not an act,
but a habit.

— Aristotle —

The sea is dangerous and its storms terrible, but these obstacles have never been sufficient reason to remain ashore… unlike the mediocre, intrepid spirits seek victory over those things that seem impossible… it is with an iron will that they embark on the most daring of all endeavors… to meet the shadowy future without fear and conquer the unknown.

— Ferdinand Magellan —

At every moment you choose yourself. But do you choose your self? Body and soul contain a thousand possibilities out of which you can build many "I's". But in only one of them is there a congruence of the elector and the elected. Only one — which you will never find until you have excluded all those superficial and fleeting possibilities of being and doing with which you toy, out of curiosity or wonder or greed, and which hinder you from casting anchor in the experience of the mystery of life, and the consciousness of the talent entrusted to you which is your "I".

— Dag Hammarskjold —

The day will come when, after harnessing
space, the winds, the tides and gravitation,
we shall harness for God the energies of love.
And on that day, for the second time in the
history of the world, we shall have
discovered fire.

— Tielhard de Chardin —

Let us never negotiate out of fear,
but let us never fear to negotiate.

— John F. Kennedy —

In vain do they talk of happiness who never
subdued an impulse in obedience to a
principle. He who never sacrificed a present
to a future good, or a personal to a
general one, can speak of happiness only
as the blind do of color.

— Horace Mann —

There are some defeats more
triumphant than victories.

— Michael de Montaigue —

One of the most tragic things I know about human nature is that all of us tend to put off living. We are all dreaming of some magical rose garden over the horizon — instead of enjoying the roses that are blooming outside our windows today.

— Dale Carnegie —

The life of a small group of people, who live
true to their convictions, does more and
more certain good than all writings. Let us,
therefore, young and old, direct all our
actions as much as possible towards the
realization of our convictions in our life.

— Leo Tolstoy —

No life ever grows great until it is
focused, dedicated, and disciplined.

— Henry Emerson Fosdick —

We must sail sometimes with the wind and
sometimes against it — but we must sail,
and not drift, nor lie at anchor.

— Oliver Wendell Holmes —

Most of the people I know who have what I want —
which is to say, purpose, heart, balance, gratitude,
joy — are people with a deep sense of spirituality...
They follow a brighter light than the glimmer of their
own candle; they are part of something beautiful. I
saw something once... that said, "A human life is like
a single letter of the alphabet. It can be meaningless.
Or it can be a part of a great meaning."

— Anne Lamott —

So deep and meaningful is the joy and the enthusiasm that is born in one's mind and heart by human love and helpfulness that it has the power to motivate for a lifetime...

You don't have to be a doctor to say or do that which puts light in a human eye and joy on a human face. Simply practice Jesus' commandment that we love one another. Go out and do something for somebody. These are the things that make happy people. Here is the one never-failing source of the joy and enthusiasm we are talking about.

— Norman Vincent Peale —

Prayer is a force as real as terrestrial gravity. As a physician,
I have seen men, after all other therapy has failed, lifted out
of disease and melancholy by the serene effort of prayer.
It is the only power in the world that seems to overcome the
so-called "laws of nature"; the occasions on which prayer
has dramatically done this have been termed "miracles."
But a constant, quieter miracle takes place hourly in the
hearts of men and women who have discovered that
prayer supplies them with a steady flow of sustaining
power in their daily lives.

Too many people regard prayer as a formalized routine of
words, a refuge for weaklings, or a childish petition for
material things. We sadly undervalue prayer when we
conceive it in these terms, just as we should underestimate
rain by describing it as something that fills the birdbath in
our garden. Properly understood, prayer is a mature activity
indispensable to the fullest development of personality —
the ultimate integration of man's highest faculties. Only in
prayer do we achieve that complete and harmonious
assembly of body, mind, and spirit which gives the frail
human reed an unshakable strength.

— Alexis Carrel —

Sorrow fully accepted brings its own gifts.
For there is alchemy in sorrow.
It can be transmuted into wisdom,
which, if it does not bring joy,
can yet bring happiness.

— Pearl S. Buck —

The universe works with you and
for you. It is not your enemy.

— David Spangler —

Love and ever more love is the only solution to every problem that comes up. If we love each other enough, we will bear with each other's faults and burdens. If we love enough, we are going to light that fire in the hearts of others. And it is love that will burn out the sins and hatreds that sadden us. It is love that will make us want to do great things for each other. No sacrifice and no suffering will then seem too much.

Yes, I see only too clearly how bad people are. I wish I did not see it so. It is my own sins that give me such clarity.

— Dorothy Day —

It's a sad day when you find out that it's not accident or time or fortune, but just yourself that kept things from you.

— Lillian Hellman —

Lord, Make me an Instrument
of your Peace.

— Francis of Assisi —

There are two ways to live life. One is as though nothing is a miracle. The other is as though everything is a miracle.

— Albert Einstein —

Know thyself; know your strengths and weaknesses;
your relation to the universe; your potentialities;
your spiritual heritage; your aims and purposes;
take stock of thyself.

— Socrates —

All the great blessings of my life are
present in my thoughts today.

— Phoebe Cary —

Good ideas and innovations must
be driven into existence by
courageous patience.

— Admiral Hyman Rickover —

Friendship is the strong and habitual inclination in two persons to promote the good and happiness of one another.

— Eustace Budgell —

When you know what your values are,
making decisions becomes easier.

— Glenn Van Ekeren —

Opportunity is missed by most people
because it is dressed in overalls
and looks like hard work.

— Thomas Edison —

Do or do not. There is no try.

— Yoda —

Perhaps the greatest social service that can be rendered by anybody to the country and to mankind is to bring up a family.

— George Bernard Shaw —

It is only through labor and painful effort,
by grim energy and resolute courage,
that we move on to better things.

— Theodore Roosevelt —

Whatever is true, whatever is honorable,
whatever is just, whatever is pure, whatever
is pleasing, whatever is commendable, if
there is any excellence and if there is
anything worthy of praise,
think about these things.

— Paul of Damascus —

Most men would feel insulted if it were
proposed to employ them in throwing stones
over a wall, and then throwing them back
merely that they might earn their wages. But
many are no more worthily employed now.

— Henry David Thoreau —

There are risks and costs to any programme of action, but they are far less than the long-range risks and costs of comfortable inaction.

— John F. Kennedy —

I have learned to use the word impossible
with the greatest caution.

— Werner Von Braum —

Before you can understand, motivate, and lead others, you must first understand, motivate, and lead yourself.

— Paul Myer —

People are unreasonable, illogical, and self-centered. **LOVE THEM ANYWAY.** If you do good, people will accuse you of selfish, ulterior motives. **DO GOOD ANYWAY.** If you are successful, you win false friends and true enemies. **SUCCEED ANYWAY.** The good you do will be forgotten tomorrow. **DO GOOD ANYWAY.** Honesty and frankness make you vulnerable. **BE HONEST AND FRANK ANYWAY.** Big people with even bigger ideas will be shot down by small people with even smaller minds. **THINK BIG ANYWAY.** People favor underdogs, but follow only top dogs. **BE THE UNDERDOG ANYWAY.** What you spent years building may be destroyed overnight. **BUILD ANYWAY.** People really need help but may attack you if you help them. **HELP THEM ANYWAY.** Give the world the best you have and you'll get kicked in the teeth. **GIVE THE WORLD THE BEST YOU'VE GOT ANYWAY.**

— Kent Keith —

I am only one; I cannot do everything, but still I can do something; and because I cannot do everything I will not refuse to do the something that I can do.

— Edward E. Hale —

Every great man, every successful man, no matter
what the field of endeavor, has known the magic
that lies in these words: every adversity has the
seed of an equivalent or greater benefit.

— W. Clement Stone —

Don't let life discourage you:
everyone who got where he is
had to begin where he was.

— Richard L. Evans —

Whether you think you can or you
think you can't, you're right.

— Henry Ford —

People who know how to employ themselves
always find leisure moments, while those
who do nothing are forever in a hurry.

— Jeanne-Marie Roland —

Do you love life?
Then do not squander time,
for that's the stuff life is made of.

— Benjamin Franklin —

To laugh often and much; to win the respect of intelligent
people and the affection of children; to earn the
appreciation of honest critics and endure the betrayal of
false friends; to appreciate beauty, to find the best in
others; to leave the world a bit better, whether by a
healthy child, a garden patch, or a redeemed social
condition; to know even one life has breathed easier
because you have lived. This is to have succeeded.

— Ralph Waldo Emerson —

Every circumstance,
every turn of destiny, is for your good.
It is working together for completeness.
God's plan for you is being perfected.
All things working together for your good
and for His glory.

— Billy Graham —

We are not permitted to choose
the frame of our destiny.
But what we put into it is ours. He who wills
adventure will experience it — according to the
measure of his courage.

— Dag Hammarskjold —

I said to the man who stood at the gate of the new year:
Give me a light that I may tread safely into the unknown!
And he replied: Go out into the darkness and put your hand
into the hand of God. That will be to you better than light
and safer than a known way.

— M. Louise Haskins —

I do the very best I know how — the best I can;
and I mean to keep doing so until the end.
If the end brings me out all right,
what is said against me won't amount to anything.
If the end brings me out wrong, ten angels swearing I was
right would make no difference.

— Abraham Lincoln —

I have a dream that my four little children will one day live in a nation where they will not be judged by the color of their skin, but by the content of their character.

— Martin Luther King Jr. —

My son, conduct your affairs with humility,
and you will be loved more than a giver of gifts.
Humble yourself the more the greater you are,
and you will find favor with God.

— Sirach —

One of the surest ways
to find happiness for yourself
is to devote your energies
toward making someone else happy.
Happiness is an elusive, transitory thing.
And if you set out in search of it,
you will find it evasive. But if you try to bring
happiness to someone else,
then it comes to you.

— Napoleon Hill —

I firmly believe that any man's finest hour — his greatest fulfillment to all he holds dear — is that moment when he has worked his heart out in a good cause and lies exhausted on the field of battle — victorious.

— Vince Lombardi —

If a man writes a better book, preaches a
better sermon, or makes a better mousetrap
than his neighbor, the world will make a
beaten path to his door.

— Ralph Waldo Emerson —

The future belongs to those who believe
in the beauty of their dreams.

— Eleanor Roosevelt —

Consciousness of our powers
increases them.

— Vauvenargues —

I expect to pass through this world but once. Any good therefore that I can do, or any kindness that I can show to any fellow creature, let me do it now. Let me not defer or neglect it, for I shall not pass this way again.

— William Penn —

Victory belongs to the most persevering.

— Napoleon —

And now here is my secret, a very simple secret;
it is only with the heart that one can see rightly;
what is essential is invisible to the eye.

— Antoine de Saint-Exupery —

Everybody can be great... because anybody can
serve. You don't have to have a college degree to
serve. You don't have to make your subject and verb
agree to serve. You only need a heart full of grace.
A soul generated by love.

— Martin Luther King, Jr. —

There is nothing more powerful than an idea whose time has come.

— Victor Hugo —

Do not be afraid.

— Jesus of Nazareth —

Do not pray for easy lives; pray to be stronger men.
Do not pray for tasks equal to your powers;
pray for powers equal to your tasks.
Then the doing of your work will be no miracle,
but you will be a miracle.
Every day you will wonder at yourself, at the richness of
the life that has come to you by the grace of God.

— Phillip Brooks —

One that desires to excel should endeavor
it in those things that are in themselves
most excellent.

— Epictetus —

I visualized where I wanted to be, what kind
of player I wanted to become. I knew
exactly where I wanted to go, and
I focused on getting there.

— Michael Jordan —

The secret of life is enjoying the
passage of time.

— James Taylor —

Compassion compels us to reach out to all living beings,
including our so-called enemies, those people who upset
or hurt us. Irrespective of what they do to you, if you
remember that all beings like you are only trying to
be happy, you will find it much easier to develop
compassion towards them.

— The Fourteenth Dalai Lama —

No one can make you feel inferior
without your consent.

— Eleanor Roosevelt —

Yesterday is gone.
Tomorrow has not yet come.
We have only today, let us begin.

— Mother Teresa —

One man scorned and covered with scars still strove
with his last ounce of courage to reach the unreachable
stars; and the world will be better for this.

— Cervantes —

Great spirits have always encountered violent
opposition from mediocre minds. The latter cannot
understand it when a man does not thoughtlessly
submit to hereditary prejudices, but honestly and
courageously uses his intelligence.

— Albert Einstein —

To love another person is to see the
face of God.

— Victor Hugo —

Be the change you wish to see in the world.

— Ghandi —

Dance as though no one is watching you.
Love as though you have never been hurt before.
Sing as though no one can hear you.
Live as though heaven is on earth.

— Souza —

Nothing is worth more than this day.

— Goethe —

Every blade of grass has its angel that
bends over it and whispers, "Grow, grow."

– The Talmud –

Go confidently in the direction of your dreams!
Live the life you've imagined.

– Henry David Thoreau –

Where there is great love, there are always miracles.

– Willa Cather –

The measure of your life
will be the measure of your courage.

– Matthew Kelly–

Let nothing trouble you. Let nothing frighten you.
All things pass away. God never changes.
Patience obtains all things. Nothing is wanting to
he who possesses God. God alone suffices.

— Teresa of Avila —

Courage for Cancer

If you know someone who is struggling
with cancer, we'd love to send them a
complimentary copy of
The Book of Courage.
Simply forward the person's
name and address to us at:

COURAGE FOR CANCER
c/o THE MATTHEW KELLY FOUNDATION
2330 KEMPER LANE
CINCINNATI   OHIO   45206
UNITED STATES OF AMERICA
E-mail: info@matthewkelly.org

*If you would like to support Courage for Cancer,
please send your tax-deducible donation
to the address above.*

Matthew Kelly was born in Sydney, Australia, on July 12, 1973. Over the past ten years two million people have attended his talks, seminars, and retreats. Against the backdrop of travel to over fifty countries, millions more have been touched by his writings and appearances on radio and television programs.

Kelly's books include *The Rhythm of Life, The Shepherd, A Call to Joy,* and *Mustard Seeds.* Collectively, his titles have been published in seven languages and have sold more than 700,000 copies.

Whether you received *The Book of Courage* as a gift,
borrowed it from a friend, or purchased it yourself,
we're glad you read it.
We think you will agree that Matthew Kelly is a most
refreshing voice in the world today, and we hope you will
share this book and his thoughts with your family and
friends.

If you would like to order additional copies
of this book or other materials by Matthew Kelly,
if you are interested in writing to the author, wish to receive
his free newsletter - *The Beacon*, would like information
about his speaking engagements, or would like to invite him
to speak at your church or to your group,
please address all correspondence to:

THE MATTHEW KELLY FOUNDATION
**2330 KEMPER LANE
CINCINNATI OHIO 45206
UNITED STATES OF AMERICA**

Phone: 1-513-221-7700
Fax: 1-513-221-7710
e-mail: info@matthewkelly.org
www.matthewkelly.org